The Bill of Rights

Karen Donnelly

rosen central
Primary Source ™

The Rosen Publishing Group, Inc., New York

Published in 2004 by The Rosen Publishing Group, Inc.
29 East 21st Street, New York, NY 10010

Library of Congress Cataloging-in-Publication Data

Donnelly, Karen J.
The Bill of Rights/by Karen Donnelly.
    p. cm.—(A primary source library of American citizenship)
Summary: Introduces the first ten amendments to the United States Constitution, commonly known as the Bill of Rights. Includes bibliographical references and index.
ISBN 0-8239-4472-7 (lib. bdg.)
1. United States. Constitution. 1st–10th Amendments—Juvenile literature. 2. Civil rights—United States—History—Juvenile literature. [1. United States. Constitution. 1st–10th Amendments.
2. Constitutional amendments—United States. 3. Civil rights.]
I. Title. II. Series.
KF4750.D56 2003
342.7308'5–dc22

                                                                                        2003013946
Manufactured in the United States of America

On the cover: Top right: the signing of the Constitution; bottom left: protesters marching through Sacramento, California, on April 29, 1997.

Photo credits: cover (background), p. 22 © The Library of Congress Rare Book and Special Collections Division; cover (top right), pp. 4, 17 (right), 23, 25, 28 © Library of Congress Prints and Photographs Division; cover (bottom left) © AP/Wide World Photos; pp. 5, 18, 21 © Library of Congress Manuscript Division; p. 6 © Bettmann/Corbis; pp. 7 (top), 20 © The Art Archive/Château de Blerancourt/Dagli Orti; p. 7 (bottom) © The Art Archive/Musée du Château de Versailles/Dagli Orti; p. 8 © The Official Records of the Constitutional Convention; Records of the Continental and Confederation Congresses and the Constitutional Convention, 1174-1789, Record Group 360; National Archives; p. 16 © 2003 Picture History, LLC; pp. 9 (top left), 9 (top right) © Joseph Sohm, ChromoSohm Inc./Corbis; p. 9 (bottom left) © Joseph Sohm, Visions of America/Corbis; p. 11 © The Library of Congress; p. 13 © Enrolled Acts of Resolutions of Congress, 1879–1999, General Records of the United States Government, Record Group 11, National Archives; p. 15 © Engrossed Bill of Rights, September 25, 1789, General Records of the United States Government, Record Group 11, National Archives; pp 19, 27, 29 © Hulton/Archive/Getty Images; p. 17 (left) © Madison, James, Federalist No. 10: "The Same Subject Continued: The Union as a Safeguard Against Domestic Faction and Insurrection," *New York Daily Advertiser*, November 22, 1787; p. 24 © Reuters NewMedia Inc./Corbis.

Designer: Tahara Hasan; Editor: Nicholas Croce

Contents

1 America: A New Country

The United States of America became a new country in 1783. The American people needed a new set of laws. The laws had to be written down and approved by the state leaders. They met in Philadelphia in 1787 to write the United States Constitution. The meeting was called the Constitutional Convention.

George Washington, Benjamin Franklin, and others are shown signing the Constitution in this painting. The painting was done by Henry Hintermeister in 1925. This signing was a historic moment in American history.

[1787]

Proposition of Col. Hamilton of New York in the Convention for establishing a constitution of Government for the United States.

1. The supreme legislative power of the United States of America to be vested in two different bodies of men; the one to be called the Assembly, the other the Senate, who together shall form the Legislature of the United States, with power to pass all laws whatsoever, subject to the negative hereafter mentioned.
2. The Assembly to consist of persons elected by the people to serve for three years.
3. The Senate to consist of persons elected to serve during good behaviour; their election to be made by electors chosen for that purpose by the people; in order to this the States to be divided into election districts. On the death, removal or resignation of any Senator, his place to be filled out of the district from which he came.
4. The supreme executive authority of the United States to be vested in a governor to be elected during good behaviour; the election to be made by electors chosen by the people in the election districts aforesaid — the authorities and functions to be as follows — to have a negative upon all laws about to be passed, and the execution of all laws passed — to have the direction of war when authorized or begun — to have with the advice and approbation of the Senate the power of making all treaties — to have the sole appointment of the heads or chief officers of the departments of finances and foreign affairs — to have the nomination of all other officers, ambassadors to foreign nations included, subject to the approbation or rejection of the Senate — to have power of pardoning

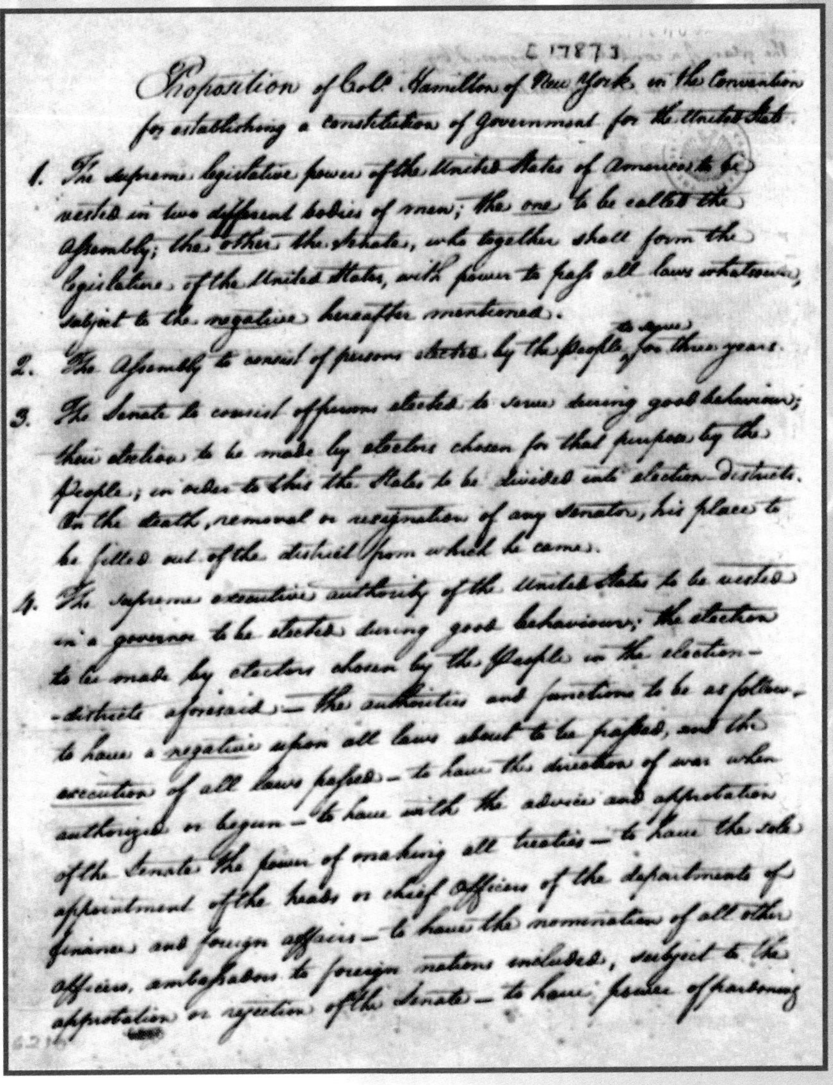

Alexander Hamilton based the Bill of Rights on state constitutions. Pictured here is Hamilton's original proposal to the Constitutional Convention. The proposal is dated June 18, 1787. This is a very important document of American history.

The meeting lasted for a total of four months. Fifty-five men from all thirteen original states, except Rhode Island, were there. These men were called delegates, and they spoke for the people of their states. The delegates were farmers, lawyers, soldiers, and merchants. George Washington, James Madison, Benjamin Franklin, and George Mason took part.

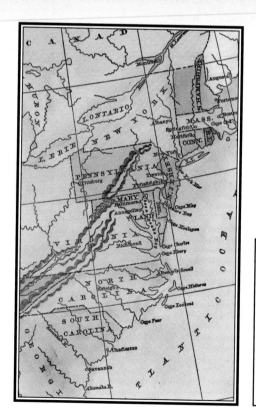

Representatives from twelve of the thirteen original colonies helped write the Bill of Rights. This map shows how the colonies looked at the time the Bill of Rights was written.

In addition to helping shape the Bill of Rights, Benjamin Franklin *(above)* was a printer, publisher, author, and scientist. George Washington *(right)* was the first president of the United States and one of the best-known people in American history.

The delegates wanted a government that listened to the people. They felt that the government they came from in Britain was unfair. The delegates decided the American government would have three branches. The president was the first branch. Congress was the second branch. The Supreme Court and other courts formed the third branch.

On May 29, 1787, the Virginia Plan was proposed. Written by James Madison, the plan outlined a national government with three branches. The branches would watch one another to prevent the abuse of power. The Virginia Plan would soon become the national Constitution.

The three branches of government were formed to watch over one another. This was to keep any one branch from having too much power. The three branches are the judicial branch *(top)*, the legislative branch *(middle)*, and the executive branch *(bottom)*. The judicial branch is the Supreme Court. The legislative branch is Congress. The executive branch is the president.

2 Setting Up the Government

The rights of Americans would be at risk if one branch grew too powerful. So the delegates worked hard to protect Americans from a powerful government. They were not sure how best to do this, though. So they made the three branches of government watch one another. This would keep any one branch from becoming too powerful.

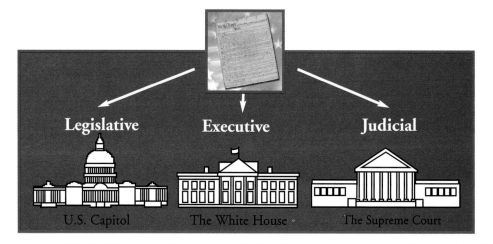

Legislative   Executive   Judicial

U.S. Capitol   The White House   The Supreme Court

The legislative branch makes the laws. The judicial branch reviews the laws and decides on court cases involving states' rights. The executive branch directs government, leads the military, deals with foreign powers, and enforces the laws.

A C T S

PASSED AT A

C O N G R E S S

OF THE

UNITED STATES

O F

A M E R I C A,

BEGUN AND HELD AT THE CITY OF NEW-
YORK, ON *WEDNESDAY* THE *FOURTH*
OF *MARCH*, IN THE YEAR
M.DCC.LXXXIX.
AND OF THE
INDEPENDENCE OF THE *UNITED STATES*,
THE THIRTEENTH.

Being the Acts passed at the First Session of the First Congress
of the United States, to wit, New-Hampshire, Massachusetts,
Connecticut, New-York, New-Jersey, Pennsylvania, Dela-
ware, Maryland, Virginia, South-Carolina, and Georgia;
which Eleven States respectively ratified the Constitution of Government for the United States, proposed
by the Federal Convention, held in Philadelphia,
on the Seventeenth of September, One Thousand Seven Hundred and Eighty-Seven.

N E W - Y O R K :

Printed by HODGE, ALLEN and CAMPBELL,
and sold at their respective Book-Stores;
Also, by T. LLOYD.

M.DCC.LXXXIX.

The first session of the First Congress met in New York from March 4 to September 29, 1789. This is the original copy of "Acts Passed at a Congress." This copy bears George Washington's signature.

The delegates decided to ask the states to approve the Constitution. They would then work on changes to the Constitution. These changes would be called amendments. The amendments would state how the rights of people would be protected. The amendments would become part of the Constitution if the states approved them.

11,000 Amendments

More than 11,000 amendments have been proposed to Congress to date. Only 27 have been approved by the states. Those 27 are now part of the Constitution.

Thirty-Eighth **Congress of the United States of America;**

At the _Second_ Session,

Begun and held at the City of Washington, on Monday, the _fifth_ day of December, one thousand eight hundred and sixty-_four_

A RESOLUTION

Submitting to the legislatures of the several States a proposition to amend the Constitution of the United States.

Resolved by the Senate and House of Representatives of the United States of America in Congress assembled, (two-thirds of both Houses concurring), That the following article be proposed to the legislatures of the several States as an amendment to the Constitution of the United States, which, when ratified by three-fourths of said Legislatures shall be valid, to all intents and purposes, as a part of the said Constitution, namely: Article XIII. Section 1. Neither slavery nor involuntary servitude, except as a punishment for crime whereof the party shall have been duly convicted, shall exist within the United States, or any place subject to their jurisdiction. Section 2. Congress shall have power to enforce this article by appropriate legislation.

Schuyler Colfax
Speaker of the House of Representatives.

H. Hamlin
Vice President of the United States
and President of the Senate.

Approved February 1, 1865.

Abraham Lincoln

This is a copy of the original Thirteenth Amendment, which made slavery against the law. It is not part of the Bill of Rights, but is similar to the first ten amendments that make up the Bill of Rights.

The delegates made it difficult to amend the Constitution. They wanted to be sure that only very important ideas were added. First, an amendment had to win the votes of two-thirds of Congress. Then, three-fourths of the state governments had to approve. The votes of nine states were needed in 1789.

Final Approval

There were three states that did not approve the Bill of Rights until 1939. The states were Georgia, Connecticut, and Massachusetts.

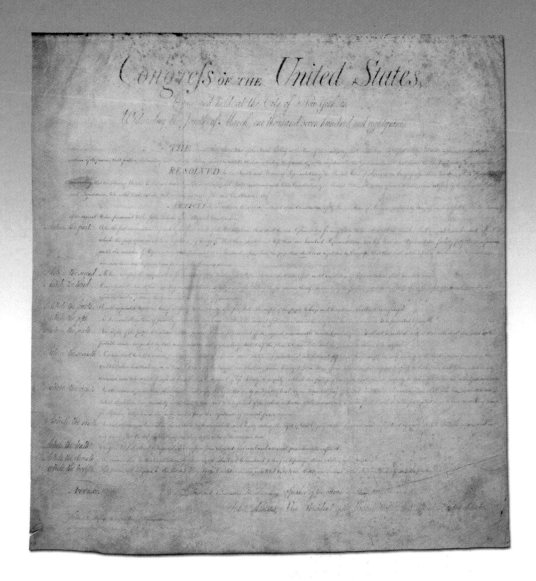

The Bill of Rights was sent to the states in 1789 for a vote. It was approved by the states in 1791. Shown here is the actual Bill of Rights document that was approved in 1791.

3

How Much Power Should the Government Have?

The delegates did not all agree on how much power the government should have. One group of delegates was called the Federalists. It thought the national government should have a lot of power over the people. Another group was called the Anti-Federalists. It felt that a national government with too much control might abuse its power.

The Federalists and Anti-Federalists did not agree on many issues about the Bill of Rights. This drawing shows that the artist believed in the Federalists. The wagon represents Connecticut filled with debts because of Anti-Federalist politics. The wagon is sinking into the mud.

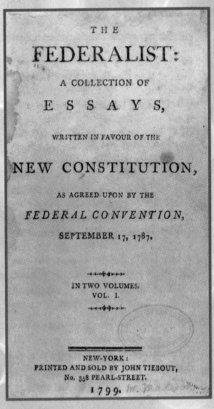

The Federalist papers were a series of 85 essays about the new Constitution and Bill of Rights. They were written by Alexander Hamilton, James Madison, and John Jay. They were published between 1787 and 1788. On the left is the tenth essay, which appeared in the *New York Daily Advertiser* on November 22, 1787. On the right is the title page of *The Federalist*, the book that was soon published containing all the essays.

George Mason was a member of the Anti-Federalist group. He wanted the Constitution to include a Bill of Rights. The Bill of Rights would give more power to the people. It would give the people rights like freedom of speech and religion. The Federalists, though, did not think the Bill of Rights was needed.

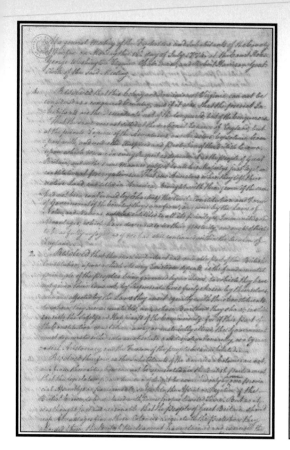

George Mason and George Washington wrote the Fairfax County Resolves on July 17, 1774, shown here. The Fairfax County Resolves was the first document to state the rights of the colonies. The Fairfax County Resolves calls for a "firm Union" of the colonies.

George Mason is one of the most important people of early American history. His ideas helped shape the Bill of Rights. Above is an etching of Mason done by Albert Rosenthal in 1888.

The states were busy deciding whether to approve the Constitution. James Madison worked on the Bill of Rights as they were deciding. Many state constitutions already had a Bill of Rights. Madison used these examples to help him write. They showed him what freedoms were important to the American people.

James Madison wrote the Bill of Rights. He eventually went on to become the fourth American president. He served as president from 1809 to 1817. This painting of Madison was done by George Healy.

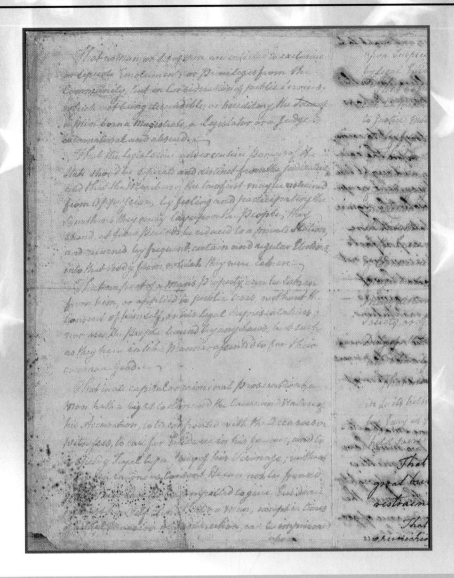

The Virginia Declaration of Rights was written by George Mason in May 1776. The document called for American independence from Britain. It was used thirteen years later by James Madison in drafting the Bill of Rights.

4 Writing the Bill of Rights

Madison began the Bill of Rights with several basic rights. They were freedom of religion, freedom of speech, and freedom of the press. Also, Americans were free to gather in groups. They were able to discuss political issues in these groups. And they were allowed to disagree with the government.

The Conventions of a Number of the States having, at the Time of their adopting the Constitution, expressed a Desire, in Order to prevent misconstruction or abuse of its Powers, that further declaratory and restrictive Clauses should be added : And as extending the Ground of public Confidence in the Government, will best insure the beneficent ends of its Institution—

RESOLVED, by the Senate and House of Representatives of the United States of America in Congress assembled, two thirds of both Houses concurring, That the following articles be proposed to the Legislatures of the several States, as amendments to the Constitution of the United States, all or any of which articles, when ratified by three fourths of the said Legislatures, to be valid to all intents and purposes, as part of the said Constitution—Viz.

Articles in addition to, and amendment of, the Constitution of the United States of America, proposed by Congress, and ratified by the Legislatures of the several States, pursuant to the fifth Article of the original Constitution.

ARTICLE the FIRST.
After the first enumeration, required by the first article of the Constitution, there shall be one Representative for every thirty thousand, until the number shall amount to one hundred ; to which number one Representative shall be added for every subsequent increase of forty thousand, until the Representatives shall amount to two hundred, to which number one Representative shall be added for every subsequent increase of sixty thousand persons.

ARTICLE the SECOND.
No law, varying the compensation for the services of the Senators and Representatives, shall take effect, until an election of Representatives shall have intervened.

ARTICLE the THIRD.
Congress shall make no law establishing articles of faith, or a mode of worship, or prohibiting the free exercise of religion, or abridging the freedom of speech, or of the press, or the right of the people peaceably to assemble, and to petition to the government for a redress of grievances.

ARTICLE the FOURTH.
A well regulated militia, being necessary to the security of a free State, the right of the people to keep and bear arms, shall not be infringed.

ARTICLE the FIFTH.
No soldier shall, in time of peace, be quartered in any house, without the consent of the owner, nor in time of war, but in a manner to be prescribed by law.

ARTICLE the SIXTH.
The right of the people to be secure in their persons, houses, papers, and effects, against unreasonable searches and seizures, shall not be violated, and no warrants shall issue, but upon probable cause, supported by oath or affirmation, and particularly describing the place to be searched, and the persons or things to be seized.

Though ten amendments make up the Bill of Rights, James Madison wrote twelve in total. These were based on George Mason's Virginia Declaration of Rights. Seen here is a copy of the first printing of the twelve amendments. This is one of only two known copies.

A Bill of Rights

as provided in the Ten Original Amendments to

The Constitution of the United States

in force December 15, 1791.

Article I

Congress shall make no law respecting an establishment of religion, or prohibiting the free exercise thereof; or abridging the freedom of speech, or of the press; or the right of the people peaceably to assemble, and to petition the Government for a redress of grievances.

Article II

A well regulated Militia, being necessary to the security of a free State, the right of the people to keep and bear Arms, shall not be infringed.

Article III

No Soldier shall, in time of peace be quartered in any house, without the consent of the Owner, nor in time of war, but in a manner to be prescribed by law.

Article IV

The right of the people to be secure in their persons, houses, papers, and effects, against unreasonable searches and seizures, shall not be violated, and no Warrants shall issue, but upon probable cause, supported by Oath or affirmation, and particularly describing the place to be searched, and the persons or things to be seized.

Article V

No person shall be held to answer for a capital, or otherwise infamous crime, unless on a presentment or indictment of a Grand Jury, except in cases arising in the land or naval forces, or in the Militia, when in actual service in time of War or public danger; nor shall any person be subject for the same offence to be twice put in jeopardy of life or limb; nor shall be compelled in any Criminal Case to be a witness against himself, nor be deprived of life, liberty, or property, without due process of law; nor shall private property be taken for public use, without just compensation.

Article VI

In all criminal prosecutions, the accused shall enjoy the right to a speedy and public trial, by an impartial jury of the State and district wherein the crime shall have been committed, which district shall have been previously ascertained by law, and to be informed of the nature and cause of the accusation; to be confronted with the witnesses against him; to have compulsory process for obtaining Witnesses in his favor, and to have the Assistance of Counsel for his defence.

Article VII

In Suits at common law, where the value in controversy shall exceed twenty dollars, the right of trial by jury shall be preserved, and no fact tried by a jury shall be otherwise re-examined in any Court of the United States, than according to the rules of the common law.

Article VIII

Excessive bail shall not be required, nor excessive fines imposed, nor cruel and unusual punishments inflicted.

Article IX

The enumeration in the Constitution, of certain rights, shall not be construed to deny or disparage others retained by the people.

Article X

The powers not delegated to the United States by the Constitution, nor prohibited by it to the States, are reserved to the States respectively, or to the people.

Regards of Harry B. Hawes.

This copy of the Bill of Rights was created in 1942. It was a gift of Senator Robert L. Owen of Oklahoma. The Bill of Rights is a very important document. This is why beautiful editions like these are printed.

The Bill of Rights also gives Americans the right to own guns. But the government is allowed to make laws to track the guns.

People also cannot be forced to let soldiers stay in their homes in peacetime. But Congress can make a law allowing this if war breaks out.

The National Rifle Association (NRA) was formed in 1871. The organization fights to protect the Second Amendment right to bear arms. The NRA is a very powerful organization. Charlton Heston, shown here, was the president of the NRA in 2000.

The Third Amendment states that no soldier can stay in a citizen's home without the approval of the owner. This was written into the Bill of Rights to protect citizens from being involved in war. Shown here is a home made for soldiers during wartime.

The government also cannot search a person's home. It can only do this with evidence of a crime.

People who are accused of a crime must have a fair trial. The trial must always happen as quickly as possible. And people cannot be forced to talk against themselves about a crime.

"Giving Thanks" for the Constitution

George Washington celebrated "giving thanks" for the Constitution on November 26, 1789. This was also the first national Thanksgiving Day.

In The Supreme Court of The United States
Washington D.C.

Clarence Earl Gideon
        Petitioner
  vs.
H.G. Cochran, Jr., as
Director, Divisions
of corrections State
of Florida

Petition for a writ
of Certiorari Directed
to The Supreme Court
State of Florida.

No. __890__ Misc.

OCT. TERM 1961
U.S. Supreme Court

To: The Honorable Earl Warren, Chief
    Justice of the United States
        Comes now the petitioner, Clarence
Earl Gideon, a citizen of The United states
of America, in proper person, and appearing
as his own counsel. Who petitions this
Honorable Court for a Writ of Certiorari
directed to The Supreme Court of The State
of Florida. To review the order and Judge-
ment of the court below denying The
petitioner a Writ of Habeus Corpus.
        Petitioner submits That The Supreme
Court of The United States has The authority
and jurisdiction to review The final Judge-
ment of The Supreme Court of The State
of Florida the highest court of The State
Under sec. 344 (B) Title 28 U.S.C.A. and
Because The "Due process clause" of the

The Fifth Amendment states that every person will be judged for a crime by due process. This means that every person has the right to a fair trial. Above is a lawsuit made in 1963 by Clarence Earl Gideon against the United States. The United States unfairly sentenced Gideon for a crime without the defense of a lawyer.

5

The Final Touches

The Bill of Rights and the Constitution could not state every right. Madison knew the documents could not list every freedom the people wanted. But he wanted to be sure the national government was not too powerful. So Madison added another amendment. It said that the states could keep the powers not written in the Constitution.

> ## Article IX
>
> The enumeration in the Constitution, of certain rights, shall not be construed to deny or disparage others retained by the people.

The Ninth Amendment states that laws not in the Constitution are given to the states. This was written into the Bill of Rights to give the states more power. Without this amendment, the government would have much more power over the people. Shown here is the wording of the Ninth Amendment.

Hon Jno G Watmough

THE

VIRGINIA AND KENTUCKY RESOLUTIONS

OF

1798 AND '99;

WITH

JEFFERSON'S ORIGINAL DRAUGHT

THEREOF.

ALSO,

MADISON'S REPORT,

Calhoun's Address,

RESOLUTIONS OF THE SEVERAL STATES IN RELATION

TO

STATE RIGHTS.

WITH OTHER DOCUMENTS IN SUPPORT OF

THE JEFFERSONIAN DOCTRINES OF '98.

"LIBERTY—THE CONSTITUTION—UNION."

PUBLISHED BY JONATHAN ELLIOT.

Washington:

MAY, MDCCCXXXII.

Here is a copy of the Virginia and Kentucky Resolutions of 1798 and 1799. It was written by Thomas Jefferson and James Madison. It allows the states to disobey the government if they find that it violates the Constitution.

The Bill of Rights has a total of ten amendments. It was sent to the states in 1789 for a vote. By December 1791, nine states had voted for the Bill of Rights. The Bill of Rights then became part of the United States Constitution. Each person's liberty would be protected by law.

Bill of Rights Day

President George W. Bush proclaimed December 15, 2002, as Bill of Rights Day. He called on all Americans to honor human rights around the world.

Glossary

amendment (uh-MEND-ment) A change to a law or rule.

Anti-Federalist (AN-ty FEH-duh-ruh-list) A person who was against the states being ruled by the federal government.

constitution (kon-stih-TOO-shun) The written laws of a country or state.

convention (kun-VEN-shun) A meeting of people to discuss a topic.

delegate (DEL-ih-get) A person chosen to act for a group.

Federalist (FEH-duh-ruh-list) A person who supported a union of states under a federal government.

liberties (LIH-ber-tees) Freedoms or rights.

national government (NAH-shuh-nul GUH-vern-mint) A ruling body with power over a group of states.

Supreme Court (suh-PREEM KORT) The most powerful court in America.

Web Sites

Due to the changing nature of Internet links, the Rosen Publishing Group, Inc., has developed an online list of Web sites related to the subject of this book. This site is updated regularly. Please use this link to access the list:

http://www.rosenlinks.com/pslac/biri

Primary Source Image List

Cover (top right) and page 4: Reproduction of a painting by Henry Hintermeister of the signing of the Constitution. This reproduction was created circa 1925 and is currently held at the Library of Congress Prints and Photographs Division in Washington, D.C.

Cover (bottom left): Photograph by Rich Pedroncelli of protesters marching through downtown Sacramento, California, on April 29, 1997.

Page 5: Original proposal for the Constitutional Convention written by Alexander Hamilton on June 18, 1787. It is now housed at the Library of Congress Manuscript Division in Washington, D.C.

Page 6: Undated map of the original thirteen colonies.

Page 7 (top): This engraving of Benjamin Franklin by Joseph-Siffr de Duplessis is currently housed at the Chateau de Blerancourt in northern France.

Page 7 (bottom): This undated painting of George Washington was done by George Healy. It is currently housed at Chateau de Versailles outside Paris, France.

Page 8: This is the original Virginia Plan drafted in 1787. It is currently housed at the National Archives and Records Administration in College Park, Maryland.

Page 9 (top left): This photograph of the United States Supreme Court was taken by Joseph Sohm circa 1990.

Page 9 (top right): This photograph of the U.S. Capitol building was taking by Joseph Sohm in April 1997.

Page 9 (bottom): This photograph of the White House was taken by Joseph Sohm circa 1994.

Page 11: Original copy of "Acts Passed at a Congress" in New York from March 4 to September 29, 1789.

Page 13: This original copy of the Thirteenth Amendment is housed at the National Archives and Records Administration in College Park, Maryland.

Page 15: This original Bill of Rights was created on September 25, 1789. It is currently housed at the National Archives and Records Administration in College Park, Maryland.

Page 16: This engraving on laid paper was created in 1787 by Amos Doolittle. It is currently housed at the Library of Congress in Washington, D.C.

Page 17 (left): This image of the original Federalist papers, number 10, appeared in the *New York Daily Advertiser* on November 22, 1787. It is currently housed at the National Archives and Records Administration in College Park, Maryland.

Page 17 (right): This original copy of the cover of *The Federalist*, volume 1, is currently held at the Library of Congress Prints and Photographs Division in Washington, D.C.

Page 18: This original copy of the Fairfax County Resolves is currently housed in the Library of Congress Manuscript Division in Washington, D.C.

Page 19: This etching of George Mason, circa 1775, was created by Albert Rosenthal in 1888.

Page 20: This portrait of James Madison was created by George Healy. It is currently housed at the Chateau de Blerancourt in northern France.

Page 21: This original Virginia Declaration of Rights is currently housed at the Library of Congress Manuscript Division in Washington, D.C.

Page 22: This original copy of James Madison's proposed Bill of Rights is currently housed in the Rare Books & Special Collections Division of the Library of Congress in Washington, D.C.

Page 23: This broadside of the Bill of Rights is currently housed at the Library of Congress Prints and Photographs Division in Washington, D.C.

Page 24: This photograph of NRA president Charlton Heston was taken by Robert Padgett in 2000.

Page 25: This lithograph of a soldier's home was created by Charles Magnus in 1868. It is currently housed at the Library of Congress Prints and Photographs Division in Washington, D.C.

Page 27: This is the original 1963 petition by Clarence Earl Gideon to the Chief Justice of the United States in the landmark case *Gideon v. Wainwright*.

Page 28: This broadside of Article IX of the Bill of Rights is currently housed at the Library of Congress Prints and Photographs Division in Washington, D.C.

Page 29: This is the original copy of the Virginia and Kentucky Resolutions of 1789 and 1799.

Index

About the Author

Karen Donnelly, a freelance writer, lives in Connecticut with her husband.